Praise For

Surviving Wonderland is a result of a mixture of diverse melancholic flavours dipped in strawberry madness. How can something deliver so much darkness and still have a bittersweet aftertaste?

Mandy has a specific magical touch only she owns. A pen only she knows how to utilise when she bleeds. Her ink is a mixture of perpetual strength, survival, and the ability to draw a unique flavour of tender madness from hurt. She brims with brilliance.

She sets the table for the reader and invites them to a rollercoaster of madness and hurt. She takes you into the rabbit hole. She pours you a tea you have not tasted before, unless you have also read her debut book *Soul Survivor*. She creates a deep longing layered in each phrase.

One will want to remain in Wonderland with her. One will want to never forget the taste delivered by this book. One will choose to sip melancholy from chipped cups at the table of her mad tea party. And cling to the satisfaction it brings.

Mandy inspires a whole new world in the reader to discover. She creates new colours and a whole new blend of magic. You will not be able to look away from her spell. She will leave a piece of her soul etched in the recesses of your palm long after you have finished reading her work.

Surviving Wonderland is a masterpiece!

S. A. Quinox,
author of *Immortalis*

In *Surviving Wonderland*, Mandy Kocsis does not cower, fearful of the darkness; her poetry proves that in fact, she wields the darkness with her white-hot brilliance. She owns her pain, and writes without apology. I believe her writing is more than a talent, it is a gift—one that she employs to inspire all who are wounded.

"I'll take my pain when I go, it's true
There won't be new memories made with you
Time will pass and wounds will scar
I'll save my soul when I leave my heart
And I promise you this; as years go by
You'll never forget the day I fly
A Phoenix lighting up the sky
The flames that'll burn with no goodbye
When you're left standing all alone
With no clue where I'm calling home."

—Phoenix Rising

Surviving Wonderland is a testament to the strength of Mandy's fire. It's a triumphant follow-up to *Soul Survivor*. Readers will be set ablaze by her use of melancholic metaphor, as well as her fierce spirit.

Kindra M. Austin,
author of *I am a war. and other poems*

Mandy Kocsis follows up her best-selling debut book, *Soul Survivor*, with a powerful and very personal collection of poetry and prose. *Surviving Wonderland* rips the bandage off every scar Mandy has. At times it's as if the rawness of her words are pouring out onto the page.

Mandy harnesses the power of her pain in pieces like 'We All Fall Down', and 'Your Move'. The words spill out from places of anger, anguish, love, empathy, and compassion. As you turn the pages, you witness her growth and almost feel the knowledge gained in each piece, especially 'Seeking Human Kindness', and 'Guardian Angel'.

Throughout the entire book, *Surviving Wonderland* provides a glimpse deep inside the author's thoughts as she shares the parts of life that have molded who she is today. Without question, *Surviving Wonderland* is a must-read if you are a fan of artists writing from a place of pure vulnerability and sharing their truth.

Jay Long,
author of *Eternal Echoes*

Surviving Wonderland is such a masterful kaleidoscope of metaphor, lyricism, and unapologetic emotion. Mandy Kocsis has outdone herself with this latest collection.

Drawing on themes of tragedy, anguish, resilience, rage, and hope, Mandy invites the reader into a world of vivid, visceral emotion and paints pictures on the soul that will not soon be forgotten.

Throughout this book, she leans heavily on imagery and metaphor reminiscent of childhood fairytales, but the trials and triumphs she writes about are not the tales from the bedtime stories.

She introduces the reader to mayhem, melancholy, and her indomitable will to survive. She weaves life lessons and a brilliant, clever brand of dry humor and sarcasm into many of these pieces; there are so many layers to this book, and there's some new treasure to be found every time you read it.

She has a unique brand of lyricism that is almost hypnotic; she is a gifted storyteller, and every piece in this book is so mesmerizing that it's easy to get lost in her words. Every piece somehow seems more captivating than the one before it, and you will be hard pressed to decide on a favourite.

Surviving Wonderland is most definitely a rabbit hole worth falling into.

Mira Hadlow,
author of *As Muses Burn*

Surviving Wonderland

Mandy Kocsis

Mandy's Land Publishing

Bloomington, Indiana

Dedication

For my mother, Teresa Kocsis,
the ultimate Soul Survivor.

Acknowledgments

A Special Thank You To:

Kindra M. Austin
Angie Waters
Ally Ricaud
Mira Hadlow
Shannon Aurelius
Jay Long
Erika Amerika
And
Rabbit

I couldn't have done it without you.
I love you all.

Contents

Surviving Wonderland

Surviving Wonderland

I've lived my life in Wonderland
It's a place like no else
Filled with darkened fairy tales
Where one must save one's self
Each journey to survival
Is different from the rest
To each one there's a lesson
And you'll have to pass a test
There's rabbit holes and rainbows
There's madness with a blade
A royal heart to kill you
And a place where dreams are made
I've lived my life in Wonderland
It's where my soul was born
And here I'll write my story
Of how I survived the storm.

Unicorns and Rabbits

Unicorns and rabbits
The world just doesn't need
More fucked up people
That think like you and me
Spreading darkness like a virus
Spreading pain like it's a seed
Losing loved one like a sports game
Knowing all we'll ever be
Just so many shattered pieces
That will never fit quite right
We never should've tried to dwell
In a world that's meant for light.

Pretty Pictures

Keep searching in that emptiness
And that's all you'll ever find
You can't create what you're looking for
Out of pictures in your mind
Of what everything should look like
And how everything should be
You lose sight of what's really real
When you lose reality
And nobody can tell you
It's a lesson you must learn
That sometimes pretty pictures
Are only good to burn.

Nightmares In the Dream

Wonderland is beautiful
Wonderland is vast
It'll kill you if you let it
It'll drown you in your past
And you won't know the difference
Between what's real and make-believe
Everything is life or death
It'll drive you to your knees
Pay attention to my warnings
I've been there many times
The last time down that rabbit hole
I barely made it out alive
Wonderland is everything
You've ever dreamed it'd be
But trust me when I tell you
There's nightmares in the dream.

Heaven In the Hell

I don't need the reminders
I remember quite well
All that came before today
The Heaven in the Hell...

This is how the angels fell.

Fake Fairytales

I thought he'd taught me everything
I'd ever need to know
About being cold and heartless
But, damn, there was room to grow
Because where he damaged my body
You damaged my soul
He only ever made flesh bleed
While you shattered every whole
He taught me that nightmares
Come shaded, dripping blood
You taught me that nightmares
Come in shades of hope and love
So when you tell our story
And you color me insane
Make sure you also tell them
You helped make me this way
For without you I'd never
Have known disdain like this
Or that the fakest of fairytales
Come wrapped in true love's kiss.

Alice: Part One

Wait a minute, Alice,
Don't fall so fast
Wonderland's a collection
Of entrancing traps
I don't believe you're ready
Please stop and think
At least pack your own
Food and drink
I've been there, you see
Where you're racing to fall
It's all you've imagined
And nothing like it at all
Nothing's like it's supposed to be
Everything's all different
So when they get to the evil part
They'll be painting the wrong villain
Enjoy your time
Learn to survive
And I'm sure you'll return
A much different Alice...in time.

A Woman Like Her

A woman like her doesn't give many chances
You're lucky to get more than one
She learned early in life
Wronged once is wronged twice
And now she generally gives none
Her soul might be battered and broken
But she's stronger than you'll ever know
And each time you hurt her
Each time you desert her
She's closer to letting you go
When a woman like her does the walking
Rest assured, you'll not see her again
Like a ghost in the night
She'll be gone from your life
Best ask yourself what you'll feel then.

Memories and Moments

It's the memories we hold onto
When all is said and done
Nothing else goes with us
No matter how we run
There's no place far enough to go
To leave them all behind
And we might wish that things were different
As they're different in our mind
It doesn't really matter, much
Where we go from here
It's the memories that sustain us
When the moment disappears.

Discover the Wonder

Discover the wonder
In each drop of rain
Explore your whole soul
Be more than your pain.

Demons and Darkness

There's things to be said
For the ones that you know
When darkness comes calling
With demons aglow
To torment your thoughts
Because that's what they do
There's things to be said
For knowing yours, too
And using that edge
To fight your way through
Each demon they send
To just fuck with you
Is one less the darkness
Will have in the end
Because I know my demons
And I've made them my friends.

Mandy Kocsis

We All Fall Down

The world had forgotten
Souls such as ours
In its rush for the easy
It lost hold of the heart
Ring around the rosy, baby
We all fall down
It's up to us to hold it up
With pocketbooks of art

Poetry and posy, baby
We all fall down
Into the ether where we never
Find our solid ground

Ashes to ashes, baby
Let the paper burn
Bleed the ink, let it sink
'Neath the flames (they'll never learn)

The world had forgotten
Souls such as ours
Till they needed escape
And sought out the arts

Now ring around the rosy, baby
We all fall down.

Mosaic Soul: Part Two

My darkness goes deeper than most people know
Survival looks good on my mosaic soul
Even lost in the darkness,
I'll STILL fucking grow
I shattered to make this beautiful whole.

Once Upon Another Life

Once upon another life
A distant Camelot
Love was more than just a dream
My broken heart forgot
And nightmares didn't wake me
With echoes of my screams
And love had yet to break me
I hadn't shattered at the seams
I wonder, now, if it was real
I ask my Goddess "why?"
I had to fall into the feel
Just to bleed, and scream, and cry
Once upon another life
For a moment, I had worth
Surrounded by his ocean eyes
Was more than I deserved
I should've known I couldn't keep him
I should've known I'm not enough
But once upon another life
For just an instant...I was loved
I didn't know what happy was
And I'll never know again
For never will I ever trust
Or let another in
Each day my soul is dying
Breath by bloody breath
I'm drowning in the memories
And I can't save myself.

Epiphany

I know why you did it, now
Though it took years to figure out
I'll admit, it was smart
To hide the truth in a broken heart...

No one ever looks there.

Mandy Kocsis

Out With Her Heart

She danced her way through Wonderland
Never thinking, "danger lurks!"
Lost in the magick of it all
Before the danger came for her.

Out with her heart!
Out with her heart!
Rip the bitch free
And tear it apart!

Thrown back into reality
Where it was all just a dream
Bleeding from that not-there heart
Danger kept that traitorous thing...

Someone should tell him it bites.

Twisted

If you want to leave my life
There's the door, stage left
Don't let it hit you when you go
I'll be just fine, myself
Got so used to it so long ago
I've no memory of a difference
People say they'll stay, then go
Like my soul has no existence
If you expect me to cry for you
You've got it all so twisted
I'll burn your very soul to ash
Like you never
Even
Existed.

Mandy Kocsis

Confused Cat

You don't understand,
Said the Cheshire Cat
No one from Wonderland
Was supposed to come back.

Fighting Wars

Days like today I have to remind myself that I fought
for this life.
I mean, clawed-my-fingers-bloody,
Do-anything-to-survive,
Ride-meets-die,
FOUGHT for this fucking life.

That there was a time in my life
When THIS life was the fairytale
I was surviving for.

Hindsight, 2020
Years after the war was over
Just a haunted battlefield
Even ghosts fear to tread
Where memories are bloody
And the nights are hell-bent

I realize how much easier it was
To fight a war
At least one of us wanted to survive.

Mandy Kocsis

Haunted

Tears on my pillow
Soaking my cheeks
Thought this part was done
And had been for weeks
But, no, there you were
In my dreams all night long
My soul knows the truth
But won't accept that you're gone
It's been almost a year
Since my world fell apart
Almost a year
Since you shattered my heart
But that's okay, baby
I'm doing just fine
Bleeding the letters
That spell out the rhymes
And someday you'll know
Someday you'll see
That your biggest mistake
Was your leaving of me
While you're out there roaming
While you're out there lost
I'm turning pain into beauty
And I'm writing the books
I told you I'd write
When you walked away
It's my name that'll haunt you
But it's my words that'll stay.

Long Lost Wonderland

It's weird, the things that stay with you
Even years after the fact
The small things you remember
After so much time has passed
The most random bits of knowledge
That no one else would know
Cuz no one else was there, then
It was just us at the show
But the weirdest thing, by far
Is finding out from you
That someone does remember
Those random pieces, too
Guess it wasn't all just me
No matter where we stand
If you remember things like that
From our long-lost Wonderland.

Mandy Kocsis

Jewelry Stars

Star light, star bright
A million tiny points of light
Scattered 'cross a velvet sky
Like a jewelry store just seen at night
There's light in every darkness
If one just looks to see
I know a thing or twelve about this
Because there's a moon inside of me.

Dancing With Death

Life is short, so love out loud
As hard as you can scream
Any day could be your last
Or it could all be just a dream
And you don't know when She's coming
Life ends in just a breath
And just like that, it's over
No one escapes Death
She's come for me, before, you know
More than once we've danced
She's whispered softly in my soul
"Love while you have the chance...
Someday, I will come for you
And someday you will know
Why I come to take you
For a spin around the floor
Just to leave without you
Without so much as a glance
You need to learn this lesson;
Love's the only thing that lasts."

Friends You Make In Fairytales

Someday I might tell you
What your friendship meant to me
At the very least, you'll find the truth
Inside my poetry
Even though it was never
A friendship built to last
You understood a side of me
No one ever has
A connection I don't think
I'll ever find again
Because I'm as done with making new ones
As we're done with being friends
I hope that you can see yourself
Inside these words I bleed
And I hope someday you understand
What it all meant to me.

No Longer Enough

Dancing with my demons is no longer enough.
Dance with my ghosts and then tell me you love me.
Swirl my dirty secrets across your tongue and
swallow them like the finest of wines. Dare my
darkness to invite you in.

Set your soul on fire.

Light my way home.

Mandy Kocsis

It's Best I Be Forgotten

And the wind in the willows
Through the wardrobe of my soul
The Lion and Witch, they console me
When the darkness takes me whole
The sidewalk ends, for me, within
It's where the wild things are
For a wrinkle in time things were different
But not since the second star
Then Neverland consumed me
Lost children aren't always found
And the Wizard tried to kill me
In life, I've often drowned
There's darkness in such tales not told
And some of us become them
Make me the velveteen rabbit, dear
It's best I be forgotten.

Bitterness of Betrayal

I thought I knew its taste quite well
I'd tasted it, before
But never here in Wonderland
Where every less is more
I knew it was a bad idea
And one that I'd regret
Still I did it, anyway
For no drink had killed me, yet
And, damn, did it taste good at first,
Like a potent blood red wine
I drank it like a losing race
Where only it could turn back time
It filled me like euphoria
It killed me like a sin
Slowly bleeding out my heart
Each time I drank it in
Then it turned acidic
Eating me alive
As I swallowed the betrayal
I didn't know if I'd survive
The pain that filled my body
The way that my soul shattered
When I swallowed down the truth
That I never even mattered.

Mandy Kocsis

Falling

I'm falling through the hourglass
I've been trapped in for so long
Full of shattered shards of me
That broke when everything went wrong
But now it seems I'm finally free
A storm of falling poetry
And for the first time, I can see
The end was always home.

Lifetimes Passed

It's been so long since I've seen you
Entire lifetimes passed
Now the space that lies between us
Is too large to get past
The lies they filled your head with
The hatred and the rage
Wrote a book upon your soul
Staining every page
I wish that I could turn back time
I wish that you could see
The truth of who I was back then
When they took you from me
But I have no magic mirror
No magic fucking wand
To pick the truth out from their lies
To show you what went on
All I can do is pray that you
Someday finally know
I never did stop looking
Just like I never let you go.

Mandy Kocsis

Recipe for Survival

Ingredients:
Determination
Steel
Fury
Will
Diamond dust
Rival
Faith

Made of determination
With a core of steel
More than a dash of fury
And a concentrated will
Dip 3 times in diamond dust
Add in any rival
Mix up well and toss with faith
And you've a recipe for survival.

Shooting Stars

You'd best learn how to fly
Or you'll never make it here
Aim straight for the sky
Shooting stars don't disappear
They wrap themselves in darkness
They fade into the night
That doesn't make them there less
Because you can't see their light
Go up in flames; use them to rise
And show 'em what you've got
Set fire to their stormy skies
And let no rain make you stop.

Mandy Kocsis

Watered Down

Never again
Will I water down my ink
For a world
That can't handle my darkness.

Karmic Hypocrisy

Hypocrisy is an ocean
She'll drown you in her depths
And you won't even notice
Till you can't save yourself
You can't hide from Karma
She sees just who you are
She knows every choice you make
That inflicts some battle scars
You might want to rethink
Hexing in Her name
Because She knows just what you're up to
She's the creator of the game
Like a spider, She lies weaving
Drawing you within
Before you can even take a breath
She'll kill you with your sins
So come at me with caution
For I'm a grey witch, too
Like Karma, I make balance
From hypocrites like you.

Mandy Kocsis

The Emerald City Is Burning

Beware the man behind the curtain
He's putting on a show
Directing his own symphony
With what he wants you to know
But things like truth and honesty
Are twisted in his view
And he's always the victim
In the tales he's spinning, too
The Emerald City is on fire
Like never seen before
And the man behind the curtain
Is the man who holds the torch
The brick road is grey with ashes
It's up to you to tell
Which way lies salvation
And which way goes to hell
The wicked witch can't save you
She's done everything she could
The Emerald City's burning
As he's laying on more wood.

Greatest Power

Peeling back the layers
Of her dark and damaged soul
Laying out the pieces
For a damaged world to hold
Is not what she'd call easy
In fact, it kills her every time
When people steal the pieces
That she lays on the line
But nothing right is easy
That's just the way it goes
They must need them more than she does
Those pieces of her soul
And so she'll keep on peeling
Though nothing left is right
Some of us were meant to be
So much more than love and light
There are those the darkness comes for
And there are those in which it dwells
So she'll scatter all her pieces
Like Easter eggs in hell
Hoping people find them
In their darkest hours
Helping them hold on to hope
And that's her greatest power.

Mandy Kocsis

Chaotic Rabbit Karma

My biggest rule I ever broke
Was believing I was loved
And I put that all on me
It's my fault just because
I should've known better
I should've listened to my soul
When it screamed you were no different
Than those that came before
But that rabbit hole was tempting
I fell before I knew
That Wonderland is suicide
Just like loving you
But that's okay, dear Rabbit,
Someday you'll finally see
Only you create your Wonderland
And only Alice has the key
Watch out for that Queen of Hearts
She'll never be enough
For chaotic Rabbit karma,
And the fear of never being loved.

Wonderland of Madness

I try not to think about the past
And the girl I used to be
But sometimes on a night like this
It's like she's haunting me
With every cracked reflection
In the mirrors of my mind
A Wonderland of madness
I'm not meant to survive
When every day's a battle
Between the present and the past
Fought on battlegrounds in my soul
In fields of broken glass
I see her blue eyes piercing me
As every soldier falls
I must murder her repeatedly
If I'm to survive at all
And the tears that blur my vision
Are every shade of red
Blood pouring from my very soul
And the me I left for dead.

Mandy Kocsis

Pretty Mouse

I am not some pretty mouse
In need of your protection
And for every rule you think there is
Baby, I'm the rule's exception
See, I know EXACTLY who I am
After years of introspection
And never have I hid the fact
I think love is just deception
Wrapped up in a pretty bow
Tied with ignorant perceptions
And don't blame me cuz you couldn't read
When I spelled out the directions.

Lies of Priceless Gold

Lies fall from your lips
Like the most priceless of gold
Like every commitment
To have and to hold
Shined up so pretty
For the world out the door
Can't have them knowing
Your words are just lore
The world is your stage
And it's all just a play
While those in your backdrop
Bleed as they pray
Cancel culture
Karma's dream
Nothing's ever
As it seems
In the darkness
Silent screams
May your lips of gold
Become the seams
And may your truth
Just end you.

Mandy Kocsis

Poetic Witch

Don't fuck with a Poetic Witch;
She casts spells directly from the Source.

The Darkest Reaches

I was born beyond the stars
In the darkest reaches of a lover's heart
Meant to shine so others see
Darkness isn't a bad thing to be
It's how you let it mold your soul
How it fills your broken whole
That's where the difference goes
I've lived for years within the light;
I killed myself to make it right
Once back in darkness, I came to see
I was born to set love free
And there's so much more to all of me.

Demented Dr. Seuss

A Dr. Seuss in a demented world
But she was born a quiet girl
Though none could see within her mind
Had no clue she's not that kind
And when she finally found her voice
Fate dictated she had no choice
Here's a pen, now write and bleed
Show them everything they need
Paint the truth on all the lies
Don't back down or compromise
Remember, they can't see your mind
They have no clue you think in rhyme
Now's the time for you to speak
You were chosen; you're not weak
The world is crazy; it needs your voice
Like Dr. Seuss, you have no choice
Poetry's not just your very soul
It's the path you'll walk before you go
All the words and all the rhymes
Wonderland leaves in your mind.

Death Wish

I fell into your ocean
I drowned inside your soul
I lost every vital part of me
When you didn't want me anymore
Every day I taste the pain
Of a soul that's slowly dying
Trapped in the flames of yesterday
And I can't escape; I'm trying
I wish I could turn back the clock
It would've never come to this
I'd make sure I never knew the love
That became death wrapped in a wish.

Mandy Kocsis

Silent Screams

They were fresh, those silent screams
That belied the brilliance of our dreams
Nightmares, daymares, dark and light
Chase us through these silent nights
Can't go forward; can't go back
When love has died, and hearts are black
Crying...trying...to forget
Each day since the day we met
Nothing left of loving dreams
Just long nights of silent screams.

Darkness & Light: Part Two

She spent a lifetime writing the same poem, and never once did she drop the pen. When life stole her ink, she opened her veins and bled. Determined to make people see, before she left this earth, that without love what is life really even worth? Although to her soul it had been nothing but a curse, still she bled all over, painting her pain out into words. Until her blood slowed to a trickle, and there was nothing left to write, she tried to make the whole world see the love that lived in light. So when her darkness came to drown her, she gave up without a fight...and finally gave up trying to ever get it right.

Mandy Kocsis

Wonderland Is Burning

Wonderland is burning
From the inside out
The very land is churning
With the hatred and the doubt
The very sky is glowing
Apocalyptic red
Ashes like it's snowing
In the nation left for dead
Wonderland is screaming
The land, once of the brave,
Is burning down to nothing
Now land just of the graves
While the Red Queen cries for ratings
And the Royal Court's corrupt
Wonderland is burning
And her land has had enough.

Funeral March

Every once in awhile
A song shuffles through my phone
Then suddenly it's years ago
And I'm back where I belong
Laughing helplessly in your arms
While you pinned me to the bed
My soul bathing in the sunlight
Of every word you ever said
But then the song is over
And I'm here all alone
Surrounded by the memories
You're everywhere; you're gone
Loneliness; a freight train
Regrets come crowding close
And all I hear is a funeral march
While I'm dancing with your ghost.

Mandy Kocsis

Soul Food

I feed my soul with "someday"
It's how we've both survived
I tell my soul that someday
This will not be our life
Someday, we'll get gone from here
Someday, we'll be free
Away from all the damage
The ghosts and memories
I feed my soul with someday
And it listens to my lies
I've known since the beginning
That this is where I'll die
Someday, I'll be good with that
Someday I'll find peace
Either way, it's a win-win
I still get to leave.

Weed, Wine, & The Cheshire Cat

It's a night for weed and wine
Usually one'll do
But on the nights like tonight
It really does take two
Take me to the stratosphere
Don't wanna feel a thing
Except the lack of gravity
And the pull of broken wings
I wanna fly away from here
I long to not look back
Cuz I'm still bleeding yesterday
Sadly, that's a fact
But there's nowhere to go
And no way to get there
So gimme the smoke, and I'll take a toke, and
POOF
I'll disappear.

Mandy Kocsis

Deadly Bliss

Ignorance is bliss...
And it's deadly.

Deadly

She walks in darkened beauty
She walks with silent flair
Strength in every step she takes
As if she owned the air
Like a Belladonna garden
With wolfsbane in the mix
As deadly as the sharpest blade
As sure as true love's kiss
You'd never guess by looking
There's no way you could know
She's so deadly that she's dying
Somewhere in her soul.

Merlot & Fleetwood Mac

Merlot and Fleetwood Mac
Poetry and wine
Bleeding in that magick ink
That always turns back time
The wine to dull the feelings
The poetry, a blade
Carving sections of my soul
In themes of yesterday
Smoky aging memories
Flowing from my pen
Rhiannon in the background
Air that's full of sin
Candles flicker silently
Flames dancing on the wall
I'm bleeding pain in poetry
And the Goddess sees it all.

Alone

We enter life alone
And we leave the same way
If we're lucky, we're loved
Somewhere on the way
But one thing is certain
Nobody can stay
This life is a journey
Everyone takes
But we're all born alone
And arrive alone at the gates
No matter your skin tone
Orientation, or faith
Your politics, your prejudice
Or what path that you take
You might want to slow down
And take a look at your soul
Is it the way that it should be
When it's your time to go?

Mandy Kocsis

Landmines

Getting lost within my mind
Not a healthy place to be
So many dark and twisted thoughts
That mock reality
Most of them are memories
I never will escape
Some are fucking landmines
That want to see me break
How much can I take, I wonder?
Before I'm really lost for good
And when I'm gone will anybody
Know I fought hard as I could?
Or will they think I just gave up?
And does it really matter?
Some of us were never meant
For happily-ever-after.

Midnight Rose

She's made of strength & moonlight
A midnight rose of thorns
You might think she's got a halo
But it's held up by some horns
Wildflowers and willows
Clovers blowing in the wind
A soul that's made for loving
With a body made for sin
She knows that she's too much for most
And alone she'll always be
She might be strength personified
And made of mystery
But it will never be enough
For anyone to stay
So while she's made of moonlight
Look closer; it's all pain.

Mandy Kocsis

The No-Sleep House

Another night at the no-sleep house
The past is way too close
Doesn't matter which way I look
I'll just see another ghost
Memories crowd in, haunting me
Bleeding, screaming, from my past
When the future looked kind of bright
And it seemed like life would last
Everyone is gone, now, though
I'm the only one that's left
On nights like this, I lack the strength
To want to save myself
Instead I drown in memories
That only I recall
I tried so hard to save each one
Just to watch each and every fall
In the end, it didn't matter
Hell, perhaps it never did
Looking back, now I can see
It would always end like this
With one left bleeding memories
O'er so many shallow graves
Carved with death inside my soul
And the memories that we made.

Not the One

I'm not the one; I don't break
I will slit your throat,
And let my tears mingle in the mess that we made
I'll walk through the blood and sleep just fine
I might remember you from time to time
But I've lost more than you'll ever keep
I've paid my price, and it was steep
I keep to myself, now
It's best that way

My darkness eats love alive.

Mandy Kocsis

Queen of Wonderland

When I first came to Wonderland
I had fallen, oh, so fast
And then it damned near killed me twice
When the worst did come to pass
But I'm not your everyday Alice
My dark side's much more dark
They know that they can't kill me, now
And I'm coming for the Queen of Hearts
I'mma take that bitch right off her throne
I'mma show her who I am
And when the blood stops running
I'll be the Queen of Wonderland.

Pick Your Poison

Pick your poison
What's your sign?
Get ready for a wild ride
Just let go
Fall from grace
There is no Heaven
And Hell's not a place
Demons, angels, all the same
And life is just a losing game
So pick your poison
Don't ask why
We all live
And we all die
It's what we do
With what time we've got
That will decide
If we were here...or not.

Mandy Kocsis

The Madhouse

The Queen of Hearts is everything
Love would never be
The Mad Hatter gives new meaning
To the word insanity
The Cat has all the answers
But disappears into thin air
The Rabbit's never what he seems
And Alice isn't always there
Wonderland's a madhouse
In far more ways than one
Stay away from rabbit holes
In fact, do better; RUN
No matter what, don't look back
There's nothing there to see
And when you get to where you're going
Pretend it was all a dream
That's the best advice I've got
If you want to survive
The madhouse that is Wonderland
Would eat your soul alive.

Mad Hatter's Tea

When the Mad Hatter
Set the table for tea
There was more than the bottles
Saying "drink me"
Napkins bleeding
Words of truth
A punchbowl of feeling
White Rabbit stew
The Mad Hatter leaves nothing,
Ever, to chance
He selected the music
To which each guest would dance
At the Unbirthday Party
Unloved for unlife
The Red Queen would say yes
And he'd make her his wife
You haven't heard evil
Until you've heard the laughter
Of a Mad Hatter plotting
To kill Ever After.

Mandy Kocsis

Darkness & Diamonds

She's made of darkness and diamonds
And never will you ever see
Nearly all of her shadows and shimmers
All she's been or will be
She's an enigma trapped in a riddle
To those on the out looking in
But she knows herself, and knows quite well
There's always some saint in the sin
For your own sake, don't try to play her
She's smarter than you'll ever know
She'll be 10 steps ahead of the words that you said
Before you realize that she's let you go.

The Rabbit's Pocket Watch

I'm running out of time
And I can hear the clock that's ticking
Counting down the time I've got left to make this work
I know I'll never make it (there's too many pieces missing)
And to a certain someone, I hope you get what you deserve
Because it doesn't have to be this hard
And I know my own worth
So when you go to bed tonight
When you close your eyes to sleep
Be thankful for everything you've got
And pray that it's not all a dream.

Soul Dance

Someday, somebody is going to fall in love with my abyss, and not run screaming from its depths like you did. They will revel in my darkness and let my demons dance them home. They will see my broken soul, and they'll have no fear to bleed. They'll cut their own soul bloody, just to dance with me.

Someday, someone is going to see the dusty images you left carved into my soul. They'll see the way you promised you'd never leave me there, alone. They'll pick up your words, and engrave them into truth...as they dance me through my darkness, and far away from you.

Someday, you'll come looking; you'll find nobody's home. Even the most meant of loves leaves when they're alone. And always, you'll remember; I'll always be your curse. The one who truly had your back, for better or for worse. And you'll wish that you could just go back, even knowing you left, first.

But I'll have danced away the melody, and left you just the verse.

The Hatter's Maddened Cup

You drank the potion of forgetting
From the Hatter's maddened cup
Poured for you by the Red Queen
With her own need to trip you up
And your ocean eyes grew clouded
From the storm it gave your mind
I watched as you forgot it all
To the Red Queen's poisoned wine
That was my first lesson
In the many ways to die
Especially in Wonderland
Where fallen villains fly
While heroes lose their minds
And nothing ever makes sense
And no one makes it out alive
I drank the potion of survival
From the Hatter's maddened cup
And I promise, I'll be standing, still
When Wonderland is dust.

Mandy Kocsis

Evil Can t Win

Pounding on each door you pass
Screaming down the hall
Blood flowing like a river
You slip, you slide, you fall
You glance behind you quickly
At the monsters getting close
Evil voices fill the air
Screaming, twisted ghosts
You know if they catch you
You'll die screaming; you'll die slow
You know they'll drain you dry, again
Then try to steal your soul
Your heart is pounding loudly
Nearly drowning out the sounds
Of bloody, soulless terror
That, EVERYWHERE, abounds
Now you're running blindly
As the evil ghosts give chase
There HAS to be an exit
Out of this Hell-bound place
Flying 'round the corner
You spot way up ahead
A square of blessed hope
Yet your soul is filled with dread
You know you'll never make it
It's too far down the hall
Then bloody bones snatch at your hair

Surviving Wonderland

And you begin to fall
Into a light so blinding
No darkness can exist
And you realize that your running
Would always end like this
A period to a sentence
A stone upon a grave
But at least you went down swinging
With every step you ever made
And you know it counts for something
Now that it's finally done
You gave your all and faltered
Yet, somehow, you still won.

Mandy Kocsis

Revolving Door

My life is not your revolving door
In and out like less is more
I'm not the girl I was before
I'm not the number to keep your score
I'm the soul you shattered, twice
Though I must admit it must be nice
To be loved like you're not made of ice
With a love that lets you break them twice
So please go back from whence you came
Remember, now things aren't the same
I'm not the one, here, playing games
But best believe I'll douse the flames
You'll not burn me one more time
Twice I let you cross that line
And you might play but I'm not that kind
Sorry, babe, it's the bottom-line
I'm not the girl you left last time.

Size Matters

I refuse to just be smaller
Than I've ever been before
You'll not have that satisfaction
You'll not change me at my core
Who I am today
And who I've always been
A larger than life poet
Who screams about the sins
This life has thrown against her
Using people just like you
I refuse to just be smaller
Because your mind is smaller, too
Remember this as years roll by
Becoming decades hence
Of us two, which one was true,
To all we've ever been.

Mandy Kocsis

Freefalling

2 bowls of green
And 2 glasses of wine
I have to admit
I'm feeling just fine
The words, they're flowing
The feelings on tap
Even if I'm freefalling
Off of the map
What does it matter now?
Each dream turned to dust
Even those made reality
Just dreams turned to rust
But it doesn't really matter
The whole world's fucked and gone
Just pass me another glass of wine
While I load another bong.

Perhaps It's Better (Fade Away)

Then there's times my soul
Doesn't have the ink to bleed
She's exhausted from the battles
In the words she's left to read
She's faded into silence
In the shadows of my mind
Hoping no one sees this pain
It's of a different kind
Than she's ever really felt before
And she can't find the words to say
Perhaps this time it's better
To simply fade away.

Mandy Kocsis

Seeking Human Kindness

Seeking human kindness
It's always been in short supply
Now, it seems it's disappeared
And didn't even say goodbye
Sometime around a year ago
The whole world lost its mind
And a "but I'm right" mentality
Replaced anything close to kind
Sometimes I'll catch glimmers
Just hints it still exists
I'm seeking human kindness
Proof we're still more than this
But my hope is slowly dying
With every day that passes
I hope I close my eyes in time
When "I'm right" hits the masses.

Something In Them Dies

With the fire burning brightly
You'd think everything's okay
The warmth is filling up the house
The predators kept at bay
Listen to me closely
And I'll tell you the way
This story really ended
On that November day
He'd been drinking like a sailor
All day while she was gone
And when she walked into the house
Everything went wrong
He came up fast behind her
She could see him in the glass
An explosion rocked her world
When he knocked her on her ass
Before she could even raise her arms
Blows rained upon her head
The blood was flowing like a river
When he left her for dead
And when she woke all she could see
Was darkness everywhere
The fire long extinguished
Blood drying in her hair
She knew that it was over
That she'd somehow survived
Now all she had to do was

Make it out the door alive
But she just couldn't find the strength
Instead she closed her eyes
For even when the good survive
Something in them dies.

Puff, Puff, Past

Nights like this I find myself
Thinking of those gone
Playing puff, puff with the past
While I'm getting slowly stoned
Nights like this my mind is just
Another haunted mansion
Filled to the brim with all my ghosts
And damn if they're not dancing
Puff, puff, goes the past
While I take another toke
In a room that once held so much love
And that might be the biggest joke
The Universe ever played
Infusing love with death
So the two who should've made it
Just couldn't save themselves.

Mandy Kocsis

The Princess & the Dragon

I am not sick,
But I am not well
I'm trapped in my body
A prison that's Hell
It's fighting against me
A battle each day
It just wants to end me
But I won't go away
The pain unlike any
You could ever imagine
If I am the princess
My body's the dragon
Lighting me up
From my hair to my toes
Each nerve ending afire
And peace is a ghost
Chronic illness a war
You can't understand
In life's game of poker
This is the hand
Most people would fold on
And just walk away
But for me the deck's stacked
There's no choice but to play
Someday I'll lose
I already know
I'll refuse to go quietly

Surviving Wonderland

When it's my time to go
For I am a warrior
And this is my fight
I'll never go quietly
Into that good night.

Karma &The Queen of Hearts

Careful, love, your hate is showing
Your soul is on the stage
And everyone can see, now
The hatred and the rage
Careful, Love, the curtain's dropped
And the spotlight's brightly trained
On the ugliness you're spreading
All the vitriolic pain
Careful, Love, She's watching, too
In all Her magick glory
And you've made yourself the villain
In this sweeping, epic story
Careful, Love, Karma's a bitch
And right now, She's taking notes
If She came for your throne, today
She'd even have our votes.

Breaking Curses

I knew that this was coming
I knew I'd hear from you
When you needed something
Because that's what assholes do
You're just forgetting one thing
You're the one that walked away
And when you did, you set me free
I'm not the one you left that day
Now you want me to save your ass
That's not my job anymore
Good luck finding solid ground
While karma sets the score
How many times must she knock you down
Before you finally see?
Only you can break the curse
You cast when you left me
Balance is an endgame
And you're hanging off the edge
Asking me to save you
Because you can't save yourself.

Mandy Kocsis

Click

You'll try replacing me
With pale shades of me
But never will they ever be
The one you're looking for
You checked that at the door
You forgot to close behind you
When you wanted something more
They'll never make your laughter
Reach down to your soul
You might find some ever after
But not the one you're searching for

In your quest for something more.

What you never understood
About what you had with me
Doesn't happen often
And it's never...EVER...free
It'll bring you to your knees
It'll cut you till you bleed
It'll take you to your limits
Like a spender on a spree...

Cuz that's the price that's due

And don't tell me that
You never knew

Surviving Wonderland

How it felt to fly
With the heights we went to
It wasn't all me
And it wasn't all you
It's the way we fit together...

When together, we flew

It's getting cold in here tonight
It's freezing in this room
I need to close that door you left
And I need to do it soon

I wish you nothing but the best
It's just a shame you lost it
But have fun playing with the rest
Goodnight, now...

I'm exhausted...

click

Mandy Kocsis

The Razor

The good news is I'm not writing about you
anymore.
The bad news is I'm not writing about anything.
It's hard to bleed when you can't feel the razor...
Only a poet begs pain to save her.

Misjudged

I'm not the one to trifle with
I can stand on what I say
I faced my demons long ago
And lived to walk away
So if you paint my name with lies
Know I'll paint yours with truth
I'm not an evil, heartless bitch
But I'll give the devil his due
And there's nothing you can do or say
That'll make me less than you
So when the hateful burn
Of the whiskey heading south
Pools within your ugly heart
Taste my name inside your mouth
Wish that you could turn back time
Misjudge me once again
And take the road you didn't take
When you lied on me to friends.

Mandy Kocsis

The Path Not Taken

I resent the path not taken
And the reasons that it calls
So many of my dreams forsaken
On the path where I was lost
Backtracking through the heartache
While trying not to drown
In the memories of my soul break
And the times I let me down
A journey full of nightmares
Landmines in my past
That tell of how I got there
On that lost and broken path
Healing isn't pretty
It's down to do or die
There's no hiding from yourself
If your goal is to survive
I resent the path not taken
But I'm grateful that it's there
I'm finding dreams forsaken
As I'm coming up for air.

The Darkness We Carry

It's true, what they say; in 7 years, I'll have a body
you will have never touched.

Damn shame you left your fingerprints on my soul.
Your mark on my mind. Living memories of
different times.

I'll remember enough for the both of us.

And for the darkness we carry, I'll shine.

Mandy Kocsis

I Had to Break

I had to break to become
Who I was born to be
I had to break to level up
Within my poetry
I had to break so I would know
How strong I really am
I had to break so I'd let go
Of all that held me back
I had to break so I could build
A palace with my pieces
I had to break so I could see
Just how strong my reach is
I had to break so I could make
A new mosaic soul
I had to break; it was the only way
I'd ever let me go
Now I stand before you
In all my broken glory
For with my broken came the words
To tell my epic story.

Dancing with Ashes

I'm tired of this dance, now
We've been doing it so long
Circling the dance floor
Of everything went wrong
You sit one out
And then return
Carrying ashes
From bridges you burned
I'm not your consolation prize
Each time your world crashes
It's time for me to leave this dance
And leave you to your ashes.

Mandy Kocsis

Dark Rainbows

She was made of rainbows
But hers glowed in the dark
You had to watch her closely
To see the colors of her heart
Once upon another time
She was brightest in the light
But that was oh, so long ago
In a far more different life
Now she's a rainbow in shades of black
Painting her colors with pain
After all the hell she's been through
She'll not glow in the light again
So if you want to find her
If you truly want to see
What beauty lies in darkness
Look closer when you look at me.

Breaking My Own Heart

The poetry is crowding close
It's crying to be heard
But I don't have the ink to bleed
My soul is out of words
At the moment, it's just silent
Like a tired, fading ghost
Locked inside the memories
That matter to it most
It can't even hear the words
The Goddess wants to say
It's locked itself behind a wall
With scenes of yesterday
While I'm looking out the window
In a room that's long gone dark
Listening to the memories
And breaking my own heart.

Mandy Kocsis

Where We Fall or Fly

I want to live a normal life
It's been too fucking long
I forgot what it was like
When the whole world wasn't wrong
When people cared about each other
It wasn't "Me! Me! Me!"
When humanity worked together
To be all that they could be
Afraid those days are gone for good
That it's too late, now, to stop it
We held our own survival
And like fidiots we dropped it
We have a lot to answer for
Trust history will remember
If we're to survive what's yet in store
We've got to work together
It's time to hush our difference
And I'm just spitting facts
If we're to save our existences
We've got to have each other's backs
It's down to now or never
It's down to do or die
It's time to work together
Here's where we fall or fly.

Building Castles

Not all brokens can be mended
Some are meant to be dissected
Cadavers in your very soul
Not every broken is ever whole
It's okay to not be alright
Sometimes darkness is the light
Begetting beauty in your mind
Falling stars of a different kind
From every dream that ever died
And every love that ever lied
I build castles with my broken
And every word life left unspoken.

Mandy Kocsis

Last Moments

Wonderland is a nightmare
But who's keeping track?
Hindsight's only an option
When someone's looking back
And time just stays hidden
Till its time has long passed
Few ever see it
It goes by so fast
I've lived in last moments
Since I was quite young
And trying to catch them
Is like chasing the sun
The secret, I've found?
To grabbing last minutes?
Is to live every moment
Like you'll always be in it
But do so with knowledge
That nothing can last
And remember that moment
When that moment's the past.

Killer Red

Been walking on this path alone
So long I don't remember
When I last watched seasons pass
With anyone, together
Nonetheless, something changed
With this turn of the wheel
I was meant to walk alone
And bleed the things I feel
A path of vibrant, killer red
For anyone to find
When they're lost and need a path
From the darkness in their mind
Someday I'll have nothing left
That's where this path will end
At least I'll have that killer red
To find me once again.

Mandy Kocsis

Like the Cursed Beast

What if, on the Other Side
Two questions seal your soul
And what if both your answers
Decide which way you go?
What if, like the Cursed Beast
In the fairytale of olde
To love and to be love
Are the things that make a soul?
And say without both answers
You're just an empty shell
Whose game might be over
Just to pinball back to hell?
For no one can advance beyond
This level of the game
Until they've loved and been loved
And known both sides of the same
In all things there is balance
But this one sets the score
And here's where it gets interesting
Cuz just one ball's in your court
The other one's not up to you
It's in another's hands
You won't know if you've been loved
Till you're waiting for the chance
To move beyond this chessboard
And whatever might come next
So live life like you ARE love
And you just might pass the test.

That Crazy Rabbit

He never asked for understanding
It was a cause as lost as he
And so not many knew him
And few as well as me
I'd watched him dance through Wonderland
For years, when it was done
I'd seen truth in all his tears
He didn't show to anyone
He lived in chronic darkness
Like the Hatter, he was mad
But there were lines within his soul
For every thought he'd ever had
See, he was taught when he was young
His light side wouldn't pay
So he locked it deep inside
But it never went away
A soul of light in darkness
In a war with heart and mind
True, he was cruel, and vengeful, too
But I saw a deeper side
In the end, I saw too much
I think that's the truth
Like the pocket watch he carries
With hands that never move
Always late but just in time
To get lost once again
He never asked for understanding

Mandy Kocsis

I never asked to lose a friend
Wonderland was split in two
It became before and after
And one might be the fairytale
But one lost all the laughter
We eye each other wearily
Across that great divide
We never asked for understanding
But we know each other's minds
Insanity's the one thing
We both couldn't leave behind.

Kill the Memories

If I could I'd kill each memory
I ever shared with you
Hide their bodies deep in my soul
And set fire to every truth
I'd burn us down to nothing
Like we never even met
If I could I'd kill each memory
But I'm not that lucky, yet
At least I've turned the feelings off
So our story has no depth
Just pictures of another time
Long before you left
But best believe I'm getting close
And someday soon you'll see
I'd do more than kill the feelings
I'd kill the memories.

Mandy Kocsis

Deceiver

I've spent so many nights
Thinking of this
When truth comes to truth
It's not you that I miss
And it's not who I was
That I'm missing, either
They didn't exist
Because you're a deceiver
So many years
I lost to a lie
An elaborate vision
You held till we died
And that's what I miss
At our story's end
The lie you created
When we became friends
None of it real
From the start to the finish
Just the things I still feel
That time won't diminish
And what does that say?
Besides I'm a dumb bitch
Believing in feelings
That shouldn't exist
But that's okay, too
I've thought about it a lot
And I'd rather be love
Than be something I'm not.

You Don t Know Me

You don't know me
You know the words that I write
And the soul that just bleeds
But you don't know me
You think I'm the one
Who'll turn a blind eye away
From the bullshit you're selling
To buy a new day
But you don't know me
I see you, now, you know
In Technicolor bright
And karma has a way
Of bringing truth to light
You think because I'm darkness
I'm the villain in the tale
What you fail to understand is
I'm the balance in the scale
Just know, now, that I'm watching
And know now that I see
And know you thought you did
But you never did know me.

The Left Behind

Grief is 14 freight trains, on different tracks, going in different directions. Grief is standing in the epicenter of my own trainyard, always braced for impact, yet never prepared. Grief is the hit I always see coming, but never avoid. It rams me with the strength and speed of a locomotive on crack. Down I go, and down I'll stay, until every boxcar has rolled over every inch of my body. Bleeding and broken, I stagger to my feet. Sometimes it's minutes before the next impact; sometimes it's days. But it's always inevitable. Just as it's inevitable that I WILL rise after each and every collision. Remember that the next time you think grief makes a person weak. We are stronger than you will ever know. We take the hits no human being wants to take. We're members of a club no one asks to join.

We're the Left Behind.

Gangsta Rap

She hears no ballads anymore
She just hears gangsta rap
Since that bullet to her soul
Killed what soft she had
She might bleed in poetry
But best not read her wrong
She'll kill you without blinking
Then go write another song
Like nothing ever happened
Like your blood don't wear her blade
Look into her winter eyes
See the monster that you made
Know the one that had your back
No longer does exist
Someday when love bleeds you out
You'll wish your bullet missed
It's already far too late
And there's no going back
Cuz she might bleed in poetry
But her soul's pure gangsta rap.

Mandy Kocsis

Personal Ghosts

Angels on my pillow
Would run from my dreams
They weren't made
For the darkest of things
I'd never allow them
To rest their wings here
My demons would break them
With not even a care
My darkness is deeper
Than anyone knows
Besides, I'm protected
By personal ghosts
14 standing ready
To bless and to slay
Are better than angels
Who'd just burn away
At a touch of my demons
With one glimpse of my past
Trust me when I tell you
Angels won't last.

The One Thing I'd Change

For the first time in life
There's something I'd change
If I could go back
And just rearrange
One night of my life
One moment in time
I'd change our beginning
So you'd never be mine
I'd murder the dreams
That we built together
The best years of my life
I'd wipe out forever
The first night you held me
And every kiss
Then you'd never be something
I'd know I should miss
The first time you held me
And slept by my side
I'd erase this whole night
And get off this ride.

Mandy Kocsis

Remember My Heart

I've never belonged here
It's time that I go
Everything's wrong here
And I can hear home
I'm telling no one
I'm just gonna go
Leave behind everything
That's broken my soul
So when you can't find me
When it's too late
Look to the north
And find Heaven's gate
Look to the horizon
With each setting sun
When darkness falls
Know I was the one
Who lit up the world
When it all went dark
When I'm just a memory
Remember my heart.

The Answer

I saw someone I used to know
For just awhile today
She came by for a visit
But said she couldn't stay
She just came to remind me
Of who I used to be
Looking in her eyes, I knew
I was seeing history
Before she left, she told me
She was proud we got this far
That she'd died not ever knowing
The strength of her own heart
I asked her why the visit
After so much time has passed
She looked at me so sadly
And said this was the last
Time I'd ever see her
But she wanted me to know
There's strength yet to discover
Before she had to go
Then she told me a secret
She was never meant to stay
She said I had to lose her
And everything that ever mattered
So I could write the ending
And give birth to Ever After
Before I could say another word

Mandy Kocsis

In one breath, she was gone
But at last, I have the answer
To why everything went wrong.

Shattered Glass

You can try to numb yourself
To your entire past
But that only works for so long
Before you're only shattered glass
You'll bleed on all around you
On everything you touch
If you don't learn to deal with
That which hurt so very much
You'll leave a trail behind you
Of all you can't outrun
Bleeding with each step you take
Until there's no more blood
You'll fall right where you're standing
With no one to help you up
Because you focused on the running
And left all you ever loved.

Mandy Kocsis

Bullshit

Do you buy your own bullshit?
I've just got to know
Cuz you're constantly selling it
And you're constantly broke
Do you think if you lay it
Down thick enough
You'll convince the whole world
You've finally found love?
Cuz we all see your patterns
And, yes, it's a thing
From one chick with a husband
To the next with a ring
Looking for love
Where it'll never exist
I swear, in the end,
It'll be me that you miss
And when the sun finally sets
On this live that I live
You'll be left with the ashes
I've no more left to give.

Freezing You Out

Are you getting a clue, yet?
I'm freezing you out
I've no more left to say
And no more left to doubt
I gave you my magick
I gave you my heart
And now, in the end,
I give you my dark
May it be enough
To drown you inside
In all of the memories
And all of your lies
And if someday you manage
To come up for air
May you drown in the knowledge
That nobody's there.

Kingdom For a Crown

I sold my dreams for pennies
You bought them for free
And when you didn't want them
Gave them back to me
In tears, I started building
With rage I made them grow
Now my dreams are priceless
I wouldn't barter them for gold
You couldn't see my vision
Completely missed my strength
And the fact that I was flying
Because you couldn't see my wings
Now you're lost in the rubble
Of the world that you brought down
While I'm flying high above you
With my kingdom for a crown.

Preach

They preach about forgiveness
The preach about my pride
They preach that I should just let go
Of wounds that bleed inside
They've never tried to understand
The view behind my eyes
Of what it's like to know that you
Should never have survived
Some things I can't put to words
Although God knows I've tried
When I've simply slipped away
And left them to their lives.

Mandy Kocsis

Maestro

This life is just a symphony
Each section is a stage
It ebbs and flows, it crescendos
With love, and pain, and rage
There's melodies of laughter
That fade away to tears
There's strings of hope and chaos
And drumlines made of fear
Trumpeters of honesty
Winds of magick change
And a Maestro that directs it all
From the front of every stage
He weaves it all together
Like the fates upon a loom
All the tragedies and triumph
The glory and the gloom
Until the symphony is over
When the final notes are played
With a bow unto the angels
The Maestro leaves the stage.

The Queen of Hearts

Her people never understood
What drove the Queen of Hearts
They only saw the cruelty
That ripped their world apart
The Red Queen had her secrets
She had her reasons, too
There were methods to her madness
Beyond the blood she drew
A Queen born in the magic
Of Wonderland, itself
The secret's not that she went crazy
But in why she lost herself
Like everyone in Wonderland
She had her part to play
She was born to be love
For everyone, each day
Like everything in Wonderland
What started as a gift
Soon became a nightmare
As it began to twist
Because she lived the dark side
Of what people "in love" did
That darkness slowly bent her mind
All the cheating, hate, and lies
Soul changing pain they left behind
Until all the good in her just died.

Mandy Kocsis

The Wishing Well

There's one poem I'll never write
Just one I'll never tell
Engraved in gold upon my soul
It's called the wishing well
With words of pain like no other
Of hope and happy, too
It's a priceless, timeless treasure
I'll never write for you
I'll will tell you the secret
It's a poem that you know
But if you want to read it
You'll have to read your soul.

I Got You

People talk about "ride or die"
Like it's the only way that's true
What you really need is one
Who's made of "I got you"
Who's got you in the good times
Who's got you in the dark
And when your soul is bleeding out
They give the blood from their own heart
I've never understood the thought
That it's all "ride or die"
Cuz anyone can crash a car
And anyone can drive
It's who's got you when the crash is done
When the world is just debris
And everything is burning down
That one's the one you need.

Mandy Kocsis

Shifted

No one spots it like a writer
When the narrative has shifted
From word one there's a difference
To the most subtly conflicted
We don't let on we know it
We just observe the soul
When vibes start hitting different
When dynamics shift the whole
It's a superpower in itself
It gives us time to think
Mark the exists from the stage
And vanish in a wink
We leave behind the echoes
In trails of bleeding words
When we write down the narrative
That your soul shifted, first.

Dying Pixie Dust

I broke a promise to myself
We both know what it was
And for a time it didn't matter
But now I think it does
I broke my own trust
Trying to get back to something
That never really was
More than a lost fairytale
Drenched in dying pixie dust
We sure made some pretty memories
In the wasted years of us.

Mandy Kocsis

Wonderland's One Rule

Real is who you run to
When everything goes south
Real is one who holds your hand
With silence in their mouth
When the roof is on fire
And the building's coming down
Real's the one who'll chance the flames
Just to get you to the ground
Even here in Wonderland
There's one fact that holds true
Only three don't come in pairs
And all would slaughter you
The Red Queen has her demons
The Hatter's just insane
The Cat cannot be quantified;
He's creator of the game
There's just one rule to Wonderland
It's how I've stayed alive
You've got to learn who's really real
Or you never will survive.

The Secret Garden

You've no clue what I keep inside
I pour my soul with care
You might think you have a clue
Based on the words I share
I promise you, you're nowhere close
To guessing what's within
Most days I bleed my poetry
But I always hold things in
Never will I give the world
The things I hold most sacred
I know they'd just destroy them
For I've spent my whole life hated
But that's okay, I'm used to it
I learned when still a child
Never give them everything
If you want to save your wild
My soul is a secret garden
Where florescent flowers grow
I bleed out all my darkness
While my light, I'll never show
I might be made of poetry
The darkest words I write
But in my deepest secret place
I'm made of blinding light.

Mandy Kocsis

Letting Go

She holds on so fiercely
You really think you'll know
But I promise you won't feel it
The day she just lets go
For she lets go just as softly
As a whisper on the wind
When she does, just know that you'll
Not find her like, again
You'll spend your whole life searching
For a love that never dies
You'll look for it in empty hearts
And every pair of eyes
In everyone you ever hold
Whoever says those words
But never will you find the love
Of the one who loved you first.

I Envy Sleeping Beauty

I envy Sleeping Beauty
I'd like to sleep for years
Wake in a world that's different
With my loved ones all right here
She didn't know what she was missing
When those decades slowly passed
She lived lost in the dreaming
With no clue what year was last
I envy Sleeping Beauty
She never knew that she was lost
She slept right through her cursed days
With no clue there was a cost
And when she opened her midnight eyes
As if no time had gone
In a world so vastly different
Yet still it sang the song
Her soul was blessed with long ago
And cursed with by the same
I envy Sleeping Beauty
She slept through all the pain.

Mandy Kocsis

The Only Constant

In life, all things are fleeting
Even once upon a time
Ever after has an ending
And the words run out of rhyme
The story's ever changing
And each time, so do you
Becoming someone different
With a different point of view
In life, the only constant
Is that you'll never know
The journey yet before you
Until you've walked the road
So do yourself a favor
Don't take it all so hard
And remember, where you're going
Isn't where you are.

Write the Pain and Live the Curse

I'm just a woman who has a way with words
And a connection to the Universe
A woman who hurts
With a pain I can't put to words
A woman who bleeds in soulful verse
To write the pain, and live the curse
For the better, for the worse
I guess it's all that I deserve
For although I might know my worth
I'm the one that love leaves first
And my God, it fucking hurts.

Mandy Kocsis

Who Are You? Do You Know?

"Who are you, do you know?"
The caterpillar asked
Blowing smoke rings through the dark
He wore menace like a mask
"Well, child," he said, "DO you know?
Tell me, what's your name?
I've not seen you here before
And now 'here' is not the same."
I know too well how Wonderland
Shifts like the sands of time
It's very nature made to make
You think you've lost your mind
I calmly told the caterpillar
"I'm who you choose to see
Big or small, short or tall,
But always, I am me."
He disappeared in just a blink
Like his smoke rings in the dark
I continued on my way
But his question left a mark
"Who are you, do you know?"
He was never asking for a name
What he was really asking was
"How crazy's your insane?"

One Last Pain To Feel

The candlelight is glowing
There's music in my ears
My mind is lost down memory lane
I don't notice all the tears
Until the ink is bleeding
Cross the paper, down in truth
It's only then, I realize
I'm crying over you
I haven't done that in so long, now
I thought that part of me had healed
But I guess that it's not done with me
There's one last pain to feel
It didn't have to be this way
From the night that you walked out
Except we had to change and grow
Into the people we are, now
And for that change to happen
We each had to break
To find out what we're made of
And learn from our mistakes
That knowledge, damn, it's bittersweet
For all its painful truth
I had to learn to stand alone
You had to learn a different view
Perhaps I'm wrong to say that
In this, babe, I'm still me
All I can do is keep it real
And write it how I see.

Mandy Kocsis

Borrowed Time

Someday you'll re-read my words
In a whole new different light
You'll see another truth inside
Each poem that I write
You'll think back on these days
Right here, and all the days before
You'll not see things from my side
But you'll see a whole lot more
You'll see each word's a domino
Tracing our whole story
From beginning to the endless
In all its guts and glory
You'll see that I was shameless
Writing every word
No matter how it made us look
No matter how it hurt
I just hope I'm still around
When that day does arrive
Because nothing's ever promised
And I'm on borrowed time.

Blessed Be the Dark Ones

Blessed Be the dark ones
They know how to shine
When life hits at its hardest
They're the ones who hold the line
They roll with the punches
Can't keep 'em down for long
While the light ones fall like dominoes
When the darkness gets too strong
There's balance in all things, it's true
And you'll find both in the night
Don't assume it isn't there
Cuz you can't see the light
It streaks through with the comets
It's there in every star
And how could you not see the moon
Shining where you are
You preach like you know better
In your world of love and light
I promise when your darkness comes
You'll fall without a fight
I think I'll take my chances
In the dark I know so well
See, what you fail to realize is
How the fallen angels fell
Blessed Be the dark ones
They'll save you in the end
When your "loving light" deserts you

And you're reaching for a friend
Think on my words the next time
You judge things you don't know
And pray the darkness doesn't eat you
When it's your time to go.

Starpath

Follow the path laid out by the stars
Long before you drew air
Close your eyes; look with your soul
It's waiting for you there
I know the journey's scary
And often lonely, too
But I promise you, it's worth it
That path was made for you
At times you'll walk with others
At times you'll walk alone
Finding pearls of wisdom
In every milestone
No matter what, keep going
And someday, you will see
You'll reach your destination
And finally be free.

Mandy Kocsis

Mirror, Mirror, On the Wall

I've been sleepwalking through my life
Preoccupied with my past
When fairy tales didn't end in blood
And love was built to last
Not so very long ago
Yet lifetimes lived since then
Dreams that turned to nightmares
And enemies from friends
I built my walls so very high
I wired them for sound
Never again would I be left
Bleeding on the ground
But now my eyes are open
And now I can finally see
The one I'm most in danger from
Is the one looking back at me
In the mirror.

Lessons Learned

To everyone there is a lesson
Above all, that they must learn
One single pearl of wisdom gained
Before they take their final turn
Round the sun in all her glory
'Neath the moon and all her light
Something you were sent to grasp
In this specific life
I know that I've learned many
And, damn, some made me bleed
But in the biggest scheme of things
This time, it isn't me
See, I've finally figured out
That I'm a lesson, too
In how to love without conditions
But the student, here, is you.

Mandy Kocsis

Kool-Aid

We all loved the Kool-Aid
That's what the problem was
We all had our favorite flavors
We all had our favorite buzz
Some of us were drinking sense
While some preferred to not
But NONE of us were drinking truth
And that's what we all forgot
Each flavor has its poison
And everyone should know
It's not how fast it kills you
But the way it makes you go
That'll be the only difference
When the universe hits "send"
After the story's finally over
And history writes "The End."

When Fallen Angels Fly

I'm tired of this life
I'm tired of living
I'm tired of the way my heart
Doesn't know when to stop giving
I'm tired of the losses
They've piled up too high
I'm tired of being left behind
While fallen angels fly
My darkness is creeping closer, now
Closer than it's been in years
It's whispering constantly
It's naming all my fears
It wants me to just give up, I know
And lay down all the fight
It wants me to embrace the dark
And go into that good night
I won't lie; I want to
More than I want to breathe
Phone call after phone call
Another one just leaves
I'm tired and I'm hurting
More pain than you can see
You'd never guess it's even there
Even looking right at me
But I promise you, I'm fighting
With everything I've got
I refuse to just lay down my soul

Mandy Kocsis

A quitter's something that I'm not
But I'm tired of the living
I'm tired of the pain
And if I don't give up and go
It'll drive me quite insane
Guess I can't win for losing
Either way, I'm done
But I'll leave my words behind me
In that, at least, I've won.

No More Happy Thoughts

There's a place between the dreaming
Where Tink still waits for Peter
In a place between the worlds
She hopes that he'll remember
But her light is growing dimmer
Her pixie dust is gone
Her life is almost over
And he's never coming home
She wonders where the pixies go
When the darkness claims their light
Are they just gone forever?
Can they come back to life?
She tries to think of happy thoughts
To find she has none left
And with that, the world's last fairy
Blinked out, and killed herself.

Mandy Kocsis

Suicidal Nights

It's that kind of night
When the end looks like an answer
To every question I ever had
To make the hurt heal faster
The door to the world that waits
Is seductive when you're breathing pain
On nights like this I'm made of lost
And even the sun is crying rain
I just want to escape, somehow
To leave it all behind
Before it takes what little's left
Before I truly lose my mind
All I've left are broken pieces
That will never fit quite right
Cutting with the memories
On the suicidal nights.

Like an Angel Seeking Sin

The dark is getting closer now
Like a storm, it's rolling in
I can feel it coming for me
Like an angel seeking sin
Though most wouldn't see a way out
They're not looking the right way
I don't run from darkness
And haven't since the day
Once upon a long ago
I got lost in my dark
But I found my way home
By following the stars.

Mandy Kocsis

Rearranged

For the first time in life
There's something I'd change
If I could go back
And just rearrange
One night of my life
One moment in time
I'd change our beginning
So you'd never be mine
I'd murder the dreams
That we build together
The best years of my life
I'd wipe out forever
The first night you held me
And every kiss
Then you'd never be something
I'd know I should miss
The first time you held me
And slept by my side
I'd erase the whole night
And get off of this ride.

Brings the Thunder

My mind goes down a dark path
When life's made of wtf
I also shine my brightest, then
With just my pen and thoughts
I tend to not say very much
I'm connecting all the dots
And I'm better with the written word
Than any said aloud
But you know this about me
And sometimes it makes me wonder
If you find ways to give me rain
Just so my pen brings the thunder.

Mandy Kocsis

Warpath

When she's on a warpath
Only a fool would come near
She fights with no mercy
She doesn't know fear
When she comes up swinging
Each hand holds a blade
Itching to cut you
For each crack you made
Inside the foundation
Of her heart and soul
She's itching to cut you
And make sure you know
What it's like to bleed from wounds
You never once saw coming
I promise, you won't win the war
So you'd better just start running.

Guardian Angel

I can just see the minute
She first drew my name
I've no doubt, in that moment
She went a bit insane
"But this one's made of darkness
How can I guide her right?
She's a soul born of the tragic Fates
While I'm a being made of light?"
With smiles all around, I'm sure
The Gods told her it'd be fine
That I was made to be hers
And she, made to be mine
I wish that I could tell her
I'm sorry for the years
Everything we went through
That brought us both right here
I'd say she did her job right
I've survived each deadly angle
For the Fates wove all the fabric
And she's just one lonely angel
It couldn't have been easy
Her journey in my dark
A guardian of love and light
She poured strength into my heart
Someday, I'd like to thank her
For everything she's done
The angel that stood by me

Mandy Kocsis

These many trips around the sun
Thank you for the good times
Thank you for the bad
Thank you for survival tips
At times they're all I had
I hope someday I'll make her proud
And she'll know why it had to be
Her to take this journey;
For she's the light in me.

Christine

In a Stephen King nightmare
Her name was Christine
Guess you cut it kinda close
To finding the same thing
A bloody stain upon your soul
She convinced you she was real
A demonic fallen angel
Lured you in with every feel
Gave you golden promises
Tied up with silver things
Stabbed a knife deep in your back
And lit it up with kerosene
I've had to watch this nightmare
From an angel's fallen view
Fallen angels and angel's fall
And only one's the truth
You asked for what my soul would say
You dared me for the words
In blood since laced with cyanide
From the one who loved you first.

Mandy Kocsis

Between the Lines

It's hard not to read between the lines
When you've read the book so many times
And every page, you've memorized
From the fall to the demise
First there was the rabbit hole
The Red Queen painted every rose
While Hatter played his crazy role
With the Rabbit shouting "gotta go!"
Then the Queen was chopping heads
Wonderland was bathed in red
And Alice came real close to dead
It's hard to re-read every word
Remembering when you read them first
Knowing this to be your curse
And hoping this time isn't worse.

Your Move

It's your move
I've done all I can
If you don't get it now
You'll never understand
That what we had was priceless
And rare to the extreme
It ended with a nightmare
But it started with a dream
Now you're out there searching
There's nowhere far enough
You're on an endless circle track
In your quest to find true love
And always you just circle back
To the place that was the start
You can't run from yourself
There is no place that far
Lessons I learned long ago
That you have yet to see
To love without conditions
Costs your soul a heavy fee
It's one that I'm still paying
And will until I die
Baby, it's your move, this time
My soul is bleeding dry.

Mandy Kocsis

Death & Darkness

There is Death, and there is Darkness
The two are not the same
As light gives birth to chaos
We're all pawns in the game
Those who claim to understand
So rarely have a clue
We're just puppets on a string
With a small and censored view
Of life and all its meaning
Of loss, and grief, and love
Not meant to know the answers
Held by the Universe above
We all just dance upon our strings
To the answers that we're given
But none of that means one damn thing
If we don't take the time to listen.

Snow White to His Hunter

The Snow White to his Hunter
Our fairy tale was dark
Poison took him far from me
Before I took back my heart
I knew when I was running
There was no going home
If I was to survive us
I'd have to do it on my own
And in the end, I was the loss
He carried to his grave
Mirror, mirror, in the wall
Show me the life we made
When his weapon was an old guitar
Our chalice, full of love
Before the water turned to wine
And destroyed both of us.

Mandy Kocsis

Wounded Butterfly

I knew a wounded butterfly
She meant the world to me
Before she stabbed me in the back
And didn't think I'd see
The truth laid out before me
In words of black or white
Just one more I don't matter
In this lonely fucking life
But it's okay, I've got this
Pain's just the way it feels
When someone really matters
And shows none of it was real
I thought I knew a butterfly
Wounded just like me
Turns out I never knew a thing
Except one more way to bleed.

I'll Never Say Die

I'm light as a feather
I'm clear as a ghost
I bleed from my soul
And I give you the most
Honest of insights
You'll ever see
I can't stand a liar
And I don't lie to me
I'm far from perfect
That doesn't exist
But my truth that I give you
Is the truest there is
From eyes that have seen
Far too much death
I know that my words
Might be all that is left
To speak for my soul
To light up the sky
There's hope in the truth
I'll never say die.

Mandy Kocsis

Still a Buster

You're shifting lanes and think you're slick
Weaving through the lines
But I'm a born racer, babe
I see it every time
You should ask yourself why we don't crash
Head-on at speeds of sound
With all that dodging, all that weaving
Those cars you race around
Cuz what you fail to realize is
I could do this in the dark
On streets we've never traveled
And never miss my mark
I know how you drift and change
I've been doing this for years
While you've been busy shifting lanes
I've always been right here.

Broken-Hearted Song

He wanted me to love again
I couldn't take that chance
Perhaps someday I'll wonder
How well we might have danced
I knew it wasn't fair to him
My heart was long since gone
My soul already danced away
To the broken-hearted song
I first heard that fateful night
So very long ago
He wanted me to love again
But I can't let love go.

Mandy Kocsis

Taking Control

I wrote my truth when I told you
All the words I'd never said
What I remembered of our ending
And what it all meant
I knew I was writing you
Out of my life
I'm not sure if you caught it
But those words were goodbye.
I meant every word
But I know my own worth
As this last year has proven
We've both been well served
With each bit of karma
We've ever deserved
I don't see your blessings
But I've sure felt your curse.
Pissed you off on purpose
Because I know you so well
By saying goodbye
In a way you can't tell
I knew you would block me
And that was my goal
But this time when you blocked me
I made sure you would know
And in so doing, I've retaken control
And took back the pieces you had of my soul.

My Dark Is Supernova

Falling through my darkness
Like an endless hourglass
Spinning like a hurricane
With stars of broken glass
Planets brightly pass me
They're pieces of my past
Made of all the cutting shards
I had to lose to last
I've long lost hope I'd ever stop
But now, I see a hand
Reaching out to catch me
Can I make him understand?
My dark is supernova
A black hole shining bright
The opposite of all he is
My dark could kill his light
I'm not the one worth saving
I'm home most in my dark
Can't change if I want to
And I'm afraid of my own heart.

Decisions, Decisions

She's making some decisions
She's thinking with her soul
She's looking to the future
The places it might go
There's so much more at stake, here
Than anybody knows
She'll die if she stays here
And she'll die if she goes
That part's long been written
In ink bled long ago
She knows it's time to listen
To the wisdom in her soul
Learned throughout her lifetimes
A painful treasure trove
She's looking to the future
Through a lens of long ago
Just one thing remains unchanged
Survival's still her goal
Even if survival means
She'll have to kill her soul.

When She Fades to Black & White

When she falls apart for the last time, she'll shatter all over your life. She'll bathe your world with her colors when she fades to black and white...she'll make sure you finally see her when she leaves you with her light. Never will you find her, but always you will see, her kaleidoscope of colors will haunt your everything.

Mandy Kocsis

Gravestone

When it's all over
Let it be said
She paid her dues
In the life that she lead
Each day more painful
Then the day was, before
And yet she kept giving
Till she couldn't take anymore
She loved from a distance
But always alone
When it's all over
Put THAT on her stone.

Thank You

Thank you for the good times
And thank you for the bad
Thank you for showing me the strength
I never knew I had
Thank you for the broken dreams
That weren't meant to come true
Thank you for introducing me
To the me left after you
Thank you for the ending
That shattered every whole
But most of all, I thank you
For the walls within my soul
For I will never hurt again
The way I bled for you
I lined them with explosives
So no one could get through
Thank you for the memories
The good times and the bad
The love and all the heartache
That nearly drove me mad
I thank you cuz you made me
Take a long hard look within
And what I saw did change me
I'll not be her again
An emptiness so empty
That it echoes in your hold
I thank you for the breaking
I needed that to fix my soul.

Mandy Kocsis

Broken Girl

For just a moment, I had you back
And it was more than just a dream
I think that's what hurts the most
In that moment, I had peace
My soul was calm within me
My heart didn't fight to beat
Your voice was right there with me
And the memories didn't bleed
I'd forgotten what it felt like
To feel like I really matter
Now I'm right back where I started
The first time that I shattered
With tears to drown an ocean
Enough pain to break the world
Grief to drive a saint insane
And I'm just a broken girl.

Too Real For This Reality

I'll never belong in a world such as this
Where friends with benefits is a goal to hit
With attitudes all, "it's just a kiss"
When my soul landed, damn, it missed.
And, still...
"Where would you have had me go?"
The pointed question from my soul
Before I can even say a word
She continues, undeterred
"Perhaps you would have preferred
A time when women went unheard
Living life like living ghosts
When a man's permission mattered most?"
I can feel the tired in her sigh
"I know you're right, but damn, I tried."
And, still...
I don't belong in a world like this
Where status updates equal bliss
Relationships are hit or miss
And sex is cheap, cuz who commits?
Guess nothing here is meant for me
I'm too real for this reality.

Mandy Kocsis

Living In the Left Behind

In my life, the grief is winning
There's not much more I can say
My mind is on a timeless loop
Stuck on scenes from yesterday
Technicolor memories
With a soundtrack of our hits
Shining brightly in the footlights
Of my mind's broken mists
When I said I'd always be here
Standing last was not the plan
Living in the Left Behind
While you crossed to Other lands
Yet that's the hand I'm holding
And the only cards in play
Are broken Kings and a broken Queen
And scenes from yesterday.

I'm Good Either Way

Remember what transpired
Last time you lost your mind
When you came back, looking
I was nowhere you could find
I took pity upon you, then
Cuz I knew the pain you felt
Watching your world go up in flames
Is a special kind of hell
But this time isn't last time
A lot has changed since then
And I promise you won't find me
Should I go "poof" again
I wouldn't take this further
You're leaning off a cliff
Cuz I've learned what things matter
And I'm good either way with this.

Mandy Kocsis

Karma's Crow

Making decisions you don't come back from
On a night when no one cares
Staring through the darkness
To find nobody's there
Takes a strength so few are made of
In this world of broken cries
Where everything is nothing
And every "truth" is just more lies
There's escaping and there's running
Sometimes they aren't the same
When the bottom just keeps coming
And even love is just a game
I'll show you what I'm made of
I told you once before
When my words are made of silence
You'll understand the war
You picked to fight your battles
Is on the losing side
I've made my decision
And I didn't even cry
You're nothing now but pieces
Of a lost and broken past
And you might think you've won
But I'll be standing last
While your karma just keeps coming
Until it grinds you into dust
You made your decisions

Surviving Wonderland

Based in a liar's lust
Where love is just a figment
That never can exist
I've made my decision
And you're not one I'll miss
I hope you learn your lesson
Before you take your final breath
The path you chose is one of endings
And no one escapes the wrath
Of karma in the end times
She'll settle all her scores
With this path you've chosen
She'll show you less is never more
I'm on my way to better things
While you're destined to be lost
In a sea of no one cares
You'll pay the final cost
You tried to lay upon me
That I did nothing to deserve
Trust karma knows the difference
And enjoy the crow she'll serve.

Dust Settles

Was it real?
That's the question I tortured myself with for over a
year. Was ANY of it real, from the first "I'm on my
way" to the last "I'm out of your life"? The love along
the way...
Were the best, happiest years of my life just another
delusion, designed to protect me from a truth I
couldn't handle?
Does it even matter?
That's the question I've been asking myself for the
last several months. If it WAS just a dream, it was
the most beautiful dream the Oneiroi ever made.
And if it was real, then for almost 3 years I was
blessed to live a life more beautiful than dreams.
And people wonder why I don't want to try to love
again. They think it's because I'm afraid of getting
hurt like that again, and sure, that's part of it.
But the reality is once you've lived the dream,
anything less is settling.
Dust settles. I don't.

The Poet Heals (Saving Grace)

The poet heals in others
That which she can't heal, herself
She helps them find direction
While she's lost in her own hell
With pain so sharp it's diamond blood
Cutting every vein
She bleeds the words she can't escape
She truly is insane
She tells herself it's worth it
A trade-off with the dark
She'll take the pain of yesterday
To show them all the stars
Before she takes her final breath
Having never been enough
Let there be a saving grace
To losing all she ever loved.

Mandy Kocsis

Bruised

I will never find someone
Who knows just what to do
With all the chaos in my soul
And the spots my soul is bruised
I'm made of too much damage
Things I never will escape
I've learned to just stop looking
I'm better off this way
There's angels in the outfield
There's demons in the dark
And I've survived enough to know
That both will break your heart
Sometimes the lonely kills me
But that doesn't change the truth
It's far better to be lonely
Than to get another bruise.

The Virus and the Vaccine

If pain is a virus
Poetry is the vaccine
Using words to inoculate
Against all life's done to me
Bleeding onto paper
Putting it in verse
Poetry is the blessing
Balancing the curse
And I would never trade it
No matter how it hurts
It's a gift to create beauty
From the pain that got there first.

Mandy Kocsis

Saving Wonderland (The Key)

Wonderland was chaos
Nothing left was right
The day had turned to darkness
Or the darkness turned the light
Alice stood in silence
She'd seen this all before
And she knew when it was over
The cost would be much more
As it had been in the past
When Wonderland turned red
The last time someone lost their mind
And started taking people's heads
The longer Alice stood there
The clearer she could see
What that ghostly Cat had meant
When he turned up at her feet
"You alone can travel
Between our worlds at will
A soul that's made of Wonderland
Trapped in a broken girl
Only you can turn the lock
Because only you can see
There's beauty in each broken
There's dark in every dream."
Just that fast, he vanished
A key left in her hand
With a note attached that read
"Here's to saving Wonderland."

Write a Love Poem

Love is on the other side of the highway out of town. The sky painted red over the lakes of my birth. It's somewhere on the Eastern seaboard. It's more graves than I care to count. Love is the losses I live with, and the hope I can't bring myself to touch.

Write a love poem, she said.

Love is the one poem I cannot write.

Mandy Kocsis

Living Ghost

I once had arms to cry in
But that was long ago
Seems like it's been lifetimes
That I've held it in, alone
It's rare I let the tears fall
Where anyone can see
Sometime in the recent years
That came to include me
I feel like if just one more falls
I'll do so much more than break
Either way, the pain will kill me
For that, too, is a mistake
Healing's at its ugliest
When your wounds will never heal
And you'd kill for an off-switch
So you never have to feel
The way they bleed on certain nights
When memories cut you close
And, somehow, everyone's just gone
Yet you're the living ghost.

Denial (Lived This Lesson)

I need to take my own advice
I need to listen to my soul
I know just what this all means
I learned this lesson long ago
Denial's a great river to float on
Until the day somebody drowns
And I recognize these rapids
Trying to pull me down
I need to focus on the swimming
I need to find dry land
Cuz this time I'm not grabbing
For the illusion of your hand
The last time left me gasping
The last time stole my breath
The last time filled my lungs with water
The last time meant my death
I need to take my own advice
I need to listen to my soul
Because I know what this all means
I lived this lesson years ago.

Mandy Kocsis

That Pocket Watch Of His

When Wonderland was at its best
With her moon and stars aligned
Every color lit the world
And there was no passing time
The Rabbit had his pocket watch
With hands that never moved
And Alice wrote the seconds
They loved beneath the moon
His dark lit up her diamonds
Her night sky was his light
They brought balance to a land
That never was quite right
I think that's why they fell apart
Not that their love just ended
But in a place like Wonderland
Even love ends up suspended
Lost within a bubble
Trapped inside the mist
Until those hands start moving
On that pocket watch of his.

I'm a Writer

I'm a writer. That means I exist on caffeine, nicotine, herbal green, and broken dreams. I'm a siphon. I feel the sadness, pain, and rage; I feel it through me to the page. I'm the too-much girl, the crazy chick; and I wield my crazy with a Bic. Too real to ever be enough, most can't handle my soul's touch. To play in my ink, and swim in my depths, takes a strength not many have. I'm learning to be okay with that.

Mandy Kocsis

Battles and Wars

We can pick our battles
But we can't always pick our wars
There comes a time you must decide
Just what you're fighting for
What side your soul can breathe on
Which cliff to jump is right
There comes a time to take a stand
And you can't always pick the fight
Sometimes we were put here
To help another see
Pieces that they're missing
In life's convoluted tree
To each choice there's a purpose
You were given to decide
Are you gonna do what's right?
Or is this where your soul dies?
Is this the bloody alter where
You want to hang your soul?
Is this the reason you were here...
Or the reason that you go?

My Room

My room is called illusion
Dark clothes on the floor
Blood dark ink on paper
A sign hanging on the door
Beware all who enter
A dragon nestles here
She'll kill you without looking
She's faced off all her fears
My room is called depression
Balled up papers on the floor
Blood dark ink upon them
Words that cut my core
My room is called conclusion
Together they spell truth
I'll rise just like the phoenix
Because that's what I do.

Mandy Kocsis

Soul Blades

I won't be a price again
For anyone to pay
I know my ass is damaged
And I know that's how I'll stay
My darkness isn't baggage
I can check in at some claim
I can't leave it cuz I want to
It doesn't work that way
I've stared at me enough to know
I've gotten really real
I've spoken with insanity
Some souls never heal
Some brokens don't have fixing
Some wounds will always bleed
I refuse to cut another
And some blades my soul needs.

Keeping Promises

Never giving up doesn't mean
Never looking down
How else are you supposed to know?
How far you're from the ground?
It means you just keep going
No matter what you see
And keep that promise to yourself
You made when you broke free
From all that didn't serve you
That tried to break your crown
When you decided standing up
Meant never backing down
Your battle isn't over
It's only strategy
To look at what surrounds you
Each time your soul bleeds.

Mandy Kocsis

Meant to Fly

Shadow-coated memories
Bloody, broken dreams
The only things left here for me
And it's time I rip the seams
Staying's not an option
When the universe says go
I learned that once upon a past
I lived once, years ago
I was never meant to stay here
In this town of lying eyes
Some things were always meant to happen
I was always meant to fly.

Cancel Culture

The Rabbit kidnapped Alice
The Hatter drugged her tea
The Queen was out to kill her
The Cat warped reality
Guess we should cancel Wonderland
And Alice from her fate
I'm sure that'll fix it all
Best hurry; this can't wait!!!
Watch out while you're running
Look up at the sky
A house might fall upon you
Where rainbows never lie
Don't forget that evil witch
She's out to steal your shoes
In a city made of Emeralds
That should be cancelled, too
Dammit, there goes Tinkerbell
Dusting Peter Pan
So he can grab some children
And fly to Neverland
Where pirates make them walk the plank
Falling to their death
We really must erase that, too
Those kids can't save themselves!!!
Everything's offensive
To somebody, somewhere
If you really want to see some change

Mandy Kocsis

Find a mirror; start right there
Cancel culture's not the answer
There's no end to that line
And if you don't believe me
Go back, re-read my rhyme
Humanity's in trouble
It's all talk without a listen
And cancel culture won't do shit
Except drown us in division.

Karma Comes Home

Karma comes home.
Sometimes covered in blood and demanding
sacrifice.
Sometimes on the wings of a butterfly whose effect
you won't see for years.
Most never see her coming, even those of us who
watch for her.
Karma always, ALWAYS comes home.

She's kind of like grief that way...

Mandy Kocsis

Goodbye Says It All

Looking forward to getting gone
Time has slowed down to a crawl
But that's okay; I've got the ball
Lined up; it's nothin' but net, y'all
Watch me move with streetwise grace
Keep up, son, you're losing pace
Watching a prize that's poison-laced
That's gonna blow up in your face
I'll be gone by then I'm sure
Every poison has a cure
Like every blessing has a curse
You're the strychnine in my verse
And leaving heals when staying hurts
You blow my phone up every day
Don't want the job but want that pay
I've just got one thing left to say
And goodbye says it all.

Going Home

"Are you really leaving?"
He asked with a glare
"Just gonna dip out?
Do you just not care?"
She looked at him softly
"There's no reason to stay
Which is a reason to go
At least, that's what they say
I look around me
At this sea of despair
I'm drowning in reasons
To get out of here
The car's all but loaded
My bags are all packed
And I've thrown 4 darts
At each tip of map
Wherever I land
Is where I'll belong
Cuz it never was here
So it's time that I'm gone."
They looked at each other
Both holding their breath
And with a sad smile
She turned, and she left.

Mandy Kocsis

Target Practice

"You're kind of a bitch, aren't you?"
She asked me with a laugh.
"With an entree made of savage,
Damn right I own that.
I'm what my life has made me
I'll straight up make you cry
I see no point in holding back
But at least I never lie
What you see is what you get
I say what's on my mind
And if you're just as real with me
I'm always down to ride
But if you ever cross me, know
That savage does exist
I'll use you like you're target practice
And rarely do I miss."

Changing Roles

I need to be less selfless
When it comes to those I love
I need self-preservation
I need to pull the rug
On all that doesn't serve me
On all who hurt my soul
This is where the ball stops
Here's where I change some roles
Demotions; they're a'coming
To the roster of my life
Grace periods are over
And I've got to get it right
Pink slips, yeah, I got those, too
Cuz some have gots to go
I can see the finish line
It's time to heal my soul.

Mandy Kocsis

The Kicker

You tell me that you're interested
Then forget that I exist
So I've made it easy for you
I'll be the point you'll always miss
I don't give many chances
You've gotten more than most
I'm not one to disturb the dead
And that's twice you've been a ghost
My feelings aren't involved, here
That assumption bit your ass
I learned well with the last dude
To keep my heart well masked
You wanna know the kicker?
It's not the fact that you forgot
But the fact that you told him, not me
That's the fact that got you blocked.

Nothing Good Survives

I look forward to the day
I get to leave you in my past
The day I dip and tell this town
You're made of kiss my ass
Nothing good survives here
In this abyss of what the fuck
I can't wait to walk away
And leave it in my dust
For every dream I made here
Another had to die
I'm not good with that trade-off
So it's time for me to fly
I know I'll take the memories
Though I'd leave them if I could
And cut you out of all of me
Just like I said I would
Something else is out there
I'll meet it down the road
The next time your world crashes
You'll face it on your own
I know you think I'm kidding
'Tis a side you've never tripped
I've never been one for goodbyes
I just leave the script
Just remember when it's burning
And you're lost inside the gates
I did all I could to save you
Before I finally walked away.

Mandy Kocsis

Burnable Bridges

I've never understood why people talk about burning bridges as though they're doing something epic. I'm only interested in bridges you can't burn. If it's burnable, it's not worth having.

Surviving Wonderland

You make your wishes at 11:11
I make mine at 3-1-3
That number's always had my back
It's the Motown Soul in me
The Soul that keeps me going
When the world wants me to drown
No matter what it throws at me
I'm not one to stay down
So when I make my wishes
The Universe can see
There's so much more than wishes
In each word that I speak
Just like there's more than numbers
In the numbers 3-1-3
Look closely and you'll catch a glimpse
Of my Goddesses and me.

Mandy Kocsis

Phoenix Rising

I'll take my pain when I go, it's true
There won't be new memories made with you
Time will pass and wounds will scar
I'll save my soul when I leave my heart
And I promise you this; as years go by
You'll never forget the day I fly
A Phoenix lighting up the sky
The flames that'll burn with no goodbye
When you're left standing all alone
With no clue where I'm calling home.

Understanding Wonderland

Everything I touch turns to tragedy.

I'm far too damaged for anyone to understand.
I've known that for years. Decades, really.

I'll never forget the moment I let myself forget that.

Twin oceans of understanding, and my God, I
drowned. Threw myself into those depths like Keanu
Reeves without a parachute.

I wasn't flying; I was falling with style.

And for the first time in my life, I was home.

But everything I touch turns to tragedy.

I could never hate you. But I will hate myself until
the day I die.

And I will live my life in the poetry of the past. In
that Wonderland of madness where, for an instant, I
was understood...and loved in spite of it.

Mandy Kocsis

The Secret Of Her Survival

There was an emptiness to Wonderland
The day that Alice left
She'd watched them all lose their minds
Then watched them lose themselves
She mourned every passing
The many loves she'd laid to rest
She wished she'd known so long ago
That Death would be her test
The Death that comes with love
And the Death that comes with dying
The Death that comes with living
And the Death with just surviving
Somehow, she'd beaten all of them
While so many, there, did not
She suffered the remembering
While Wonderland forgot
The Red Queen lured the Rabbit
To a truly bitter end
The Hatter lost his battle
For the tea was not his friend
The Caterpillar choked on smoke
That spelled out "who are you?"
That bloody Cat just disappeared
Cuz that's what felines do
Alice fought with everything
She had worth fighting for
Until the day she chose to live

And wouldn't, anymore
That truly is the secret
To how Alice did survive
She possessed the purest heart
So she left that land alive.

Mandy Kocsis is a poet with a dark soul and a commitment to healing. Determined to be more than the nightmares she's lived, she bleeds her darkness into beauty and gives it to the world. The author of "Soul Survivor" also has an affinity for all things Wonderland and magic. She knows there is light in the darkness, if only one knows where to look. Born and raised in Detroit, Michigan, Mandy Kocsis currently resides with her family in southern Indiana.

You can find her books on Amazon, Barnes & Noble, The Book Depository, and other major online retailers.

Follow her at:
@Mandy's Land on Fb
@mandys_land_poetry on IG
@MandyKocsis on Twitter
@mandys_land_poetry on TikTok

Check out her website www.mandysland.com where you can join Mandy's email list!

Made in the USA
Monee, IL
23 February 2022

91720184R00125